FABRIC SCRAP BAG MAKING FOR NOVICE

A Thorough Guide in Making Bags from Fabric Scrap

TRACY BERTH

Table of Content

Chapter one
Introduction to Scrap Bags Making

How to Make a Coiled Tote Bag by Twisting Rope

Let's face it: even if you already have a closet full of totes, it can be difficult to say no to a new one. Additionally, you might require the ideal one for that brand-new outfit you have been wanting to wear. Did you know that rope can be used to create a tote bag? Yes, that's correct. This contemporary bag can be made with just a clothesline and some thread. You can still get to work even if all of your sewing experience consists of sewing straight lines. The perfect new bag is complete with a few on-trend tassels as the finishing touch.

What You Will Need

*200 feet of 1/4-inch cotton clothesline

*five spools of desired-color thread

*a 100/16 sewing machine needle

*measuring tape

*pins

*scissors

*Tassels require 6 skeins of embroidery thread (opional)

Step 1: Make the Tote Bag's Base

The rope should be folded in half at a distance of 12 inches. Start sewing with a zigzag stitch at the fold, grabbing both ropes in each thread as you go.

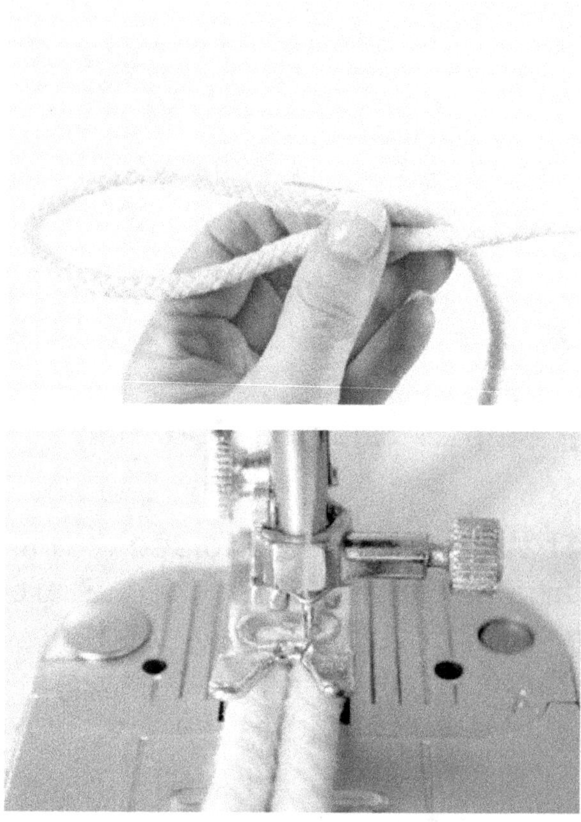

Leave the needle in the rope at the end and slowly turn the strip so that you are sewing along the curved edge as you do so.

As you continue to rotate and sew the strip, an oval will be formed, serving as the bag's base. Once you've sewed 20 rounds, stop.

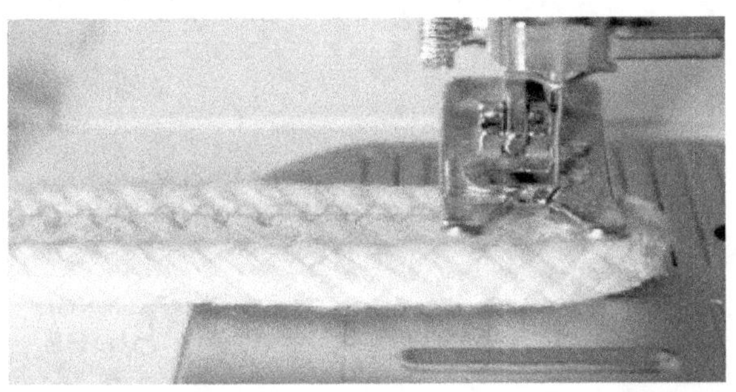

step 2: Change the thread in

Change the thread in your machine to your preferred color

before beginning to sew the
sides of your tote.

Step 3: Make the Tote's Sides

Begin by sewing a few zigzags, and after that, tilt the bag's base in a correct angle. At a sharp angle, fasten your rope. As you keep sewing, maintain a 90-degree angle with the bag's bottom. After sewing seven or eight rope coils, switch your thread color to achieve the ombre effect.

Step 4: Increase the Rope

When your rope runs out, lean the beginning of a new rope up against the end of the previous rope and keep sewing. To strengthen the seam, make a few forward and backward stitches.

Step 5: Create the handles

Stop sewing at the curved section when the height of your bag is the desired height, but leave the rope attached. Measure in at about 4 inches from each side after pinching the bag in half. Use 4 pins to mark. Your handles will begin and stop here.

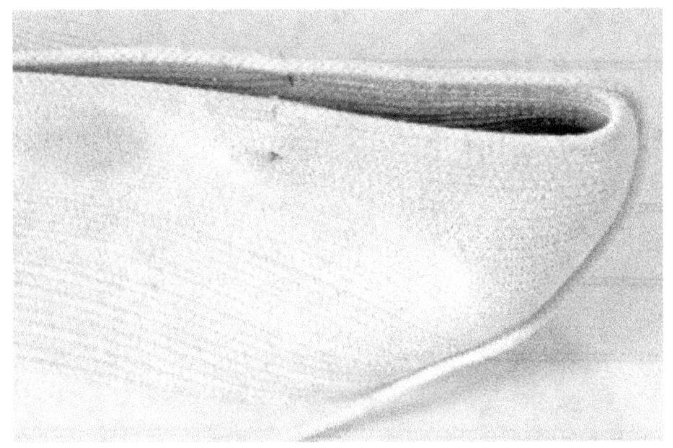

Sew all the way around until you reach the pin. To strengthen the handle, make a few forward and backward stitches. Stop sewing, take the bag out of the machine, and gauge the rope's length at 27 inches. At the following pin, reattach the rope, then begin sewing in a zigzag pattern. Measure the same amount of rope for the handle on the opposite side of the bag and repeat the process.

Continue sewing along the handle once you've gone all the way around the bag and are back at the first handle. Up until the handles are three rows thick, repeat the procedure. Trim the rope and sew a few forward and backward stitches to hold the end in place after sewing the final row on the final handle. Sew a few more inches along the top of the bag.

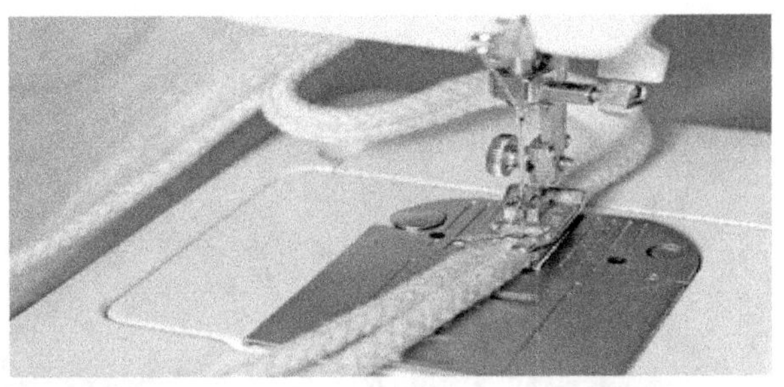

Step 6: Create the Tassels

Add some tassels created from embroidery thread in a color that complements the ombre effect of the tote to give your bag some personality.

Exactly in the middle of two full skeins of embroidery thread, tuck a 7-inch length of thread and double-knot it.

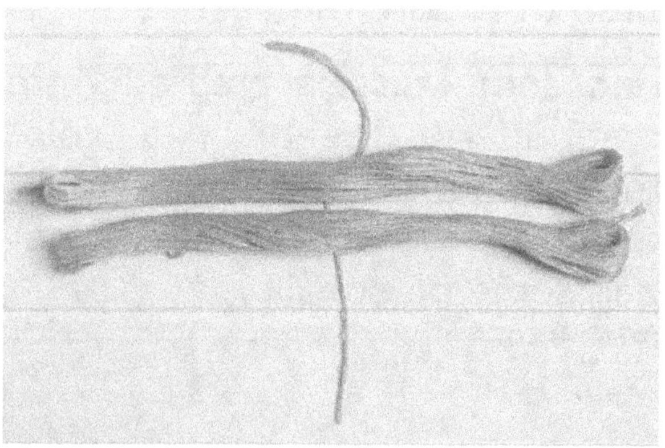

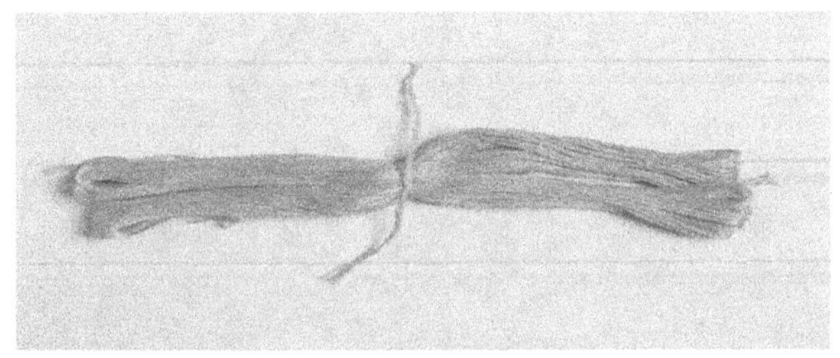

The double knot should be at the top after folding the skeins in half. The head of the tassel is formed by wrapping and tying another length of 7-inch thread around the top. Trim the ends of your tassel to give it a new look. After that, fasten the bag's tassel.

Step 7:

Pack Your Bag

Take your tote bag on weekend excursions now that it is finished.

Chapter two

How to Convert an Old Sweater into a Bucket Bag

When you arrive at the ski lodge with your winter gear in this adorable and snug bag made from an old sweater, you'll be the talk of the resort. You may proudly say that you produced it yourself when someone approaches you and inquires about which upscale ski shop offers them. To construct this purse in about an hour, all you need is an old sweater from your wardrobe or the closest thrift shop, some curtain grommets from the notions aisle of the fabric store, and an old belt.

What You Will Need

*Sharp scissors

* a sweater

* pins

*measuring tape

*curtain grommet

*markers

* a belt

*a leather needle (110/18)

* cord.

Step 1: Cut the sweater's bottom off.

Step 2: Flip the sweater inside out and sew the raw sides of the bottom together.

Step 3: Sew a 1/2-inch seam around the sweater's pinned edge.

Step 4:

To make a right triangle, align the side seam with the bottom seam. From the corner, measure 4 inches in, then pin straight down. The sewing line will be created along this.

Step 5:

 As you stitch, make careful to take the pins out.

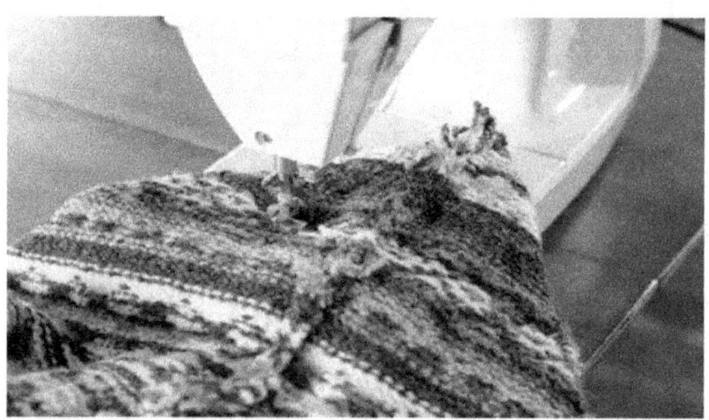

Step 6:

Trim the stitching away by 1/2 inch.

Step 7:

The grommets should be equally spaced, 2 to 3 inches below the top edge, using the tape measure as a guide.

Step 8:

Mark the grommet cutting hole on the template provided with the curtain grommets using a marker.

Step 9:

Use a pair of razor-sharp scissors to cut the grommet hole.

Step 10:

In order to capture the edge of the sweater between the two

grommet pieces, position the bottom of the grommet beneath the hole and the top of the grommet over the hole. For each grommet, repeat this procedure.

Step 11:

Position the belt's end against the edge of the bag and stitch it in place gradually using a leather needle (110/18). To attach the belt handle to the bag, you might need to use your machine's hand wheel.

Step 12:

Tighten the top of the bag by threading some cord through the grommets.

You are now prepared to give any ensemble some real winter style!

Chapter Three

Making a Bag with Leftover Fabric and Cotton Cord

I created this lovely boho bag for summer with some leftover fabric and cotton cord. You could build so many different varieties using this straightforward procedure, and it was both entertaining and simple to construct. bits of cotton fabric machine for stitching cotton cord huge thread spool, large buttons, rotary cutters, and straight pins

wafer-thin wax

Stage 1:

cut the strips.

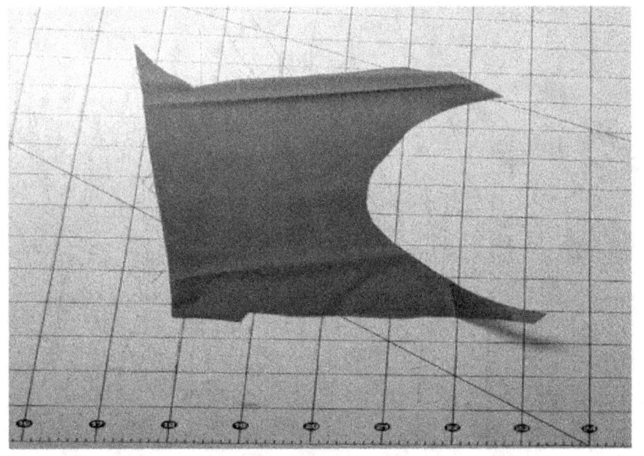

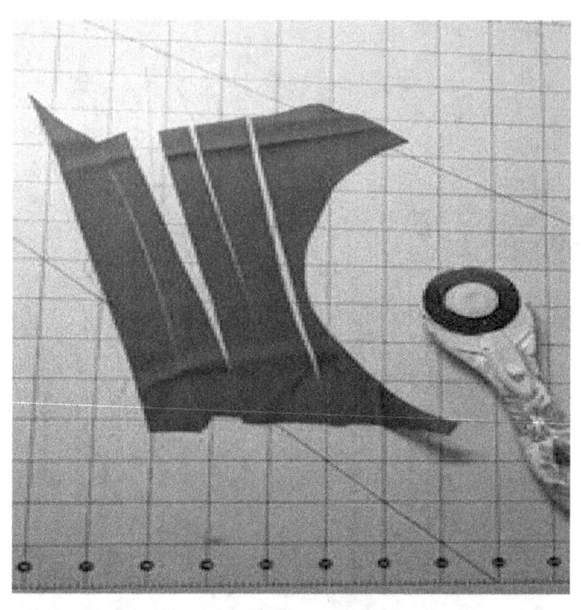

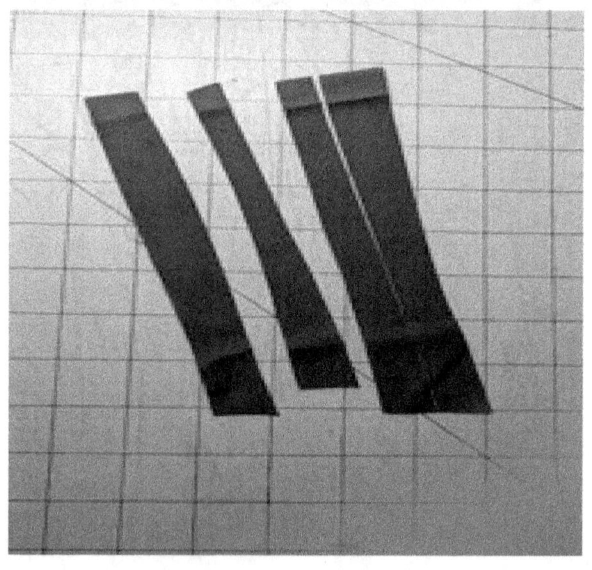

Cut leftovers into strips that range in width from 1/2" to 3/4".

After you've divided your strips into smaller pieces, combine them all so you may pick designs at random.

Stage 2:

Begin wrapping.

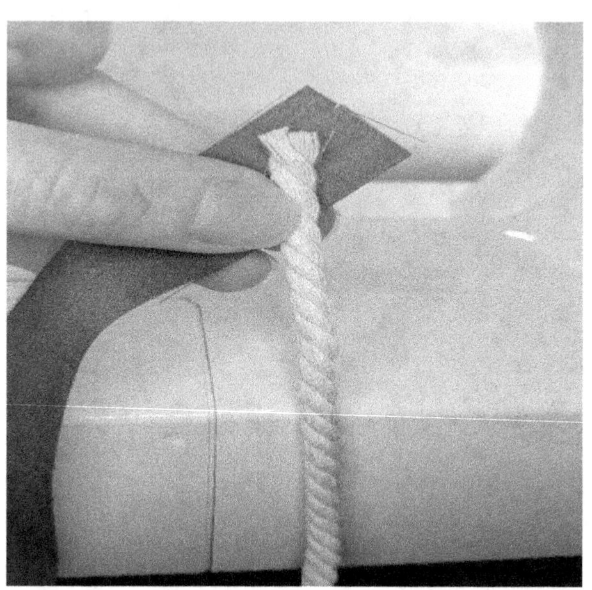

As shown, wrap the first strip around the cotton cord's end, and then zigzag stitch it in place.

Stage 3:

Keep going Wrapping

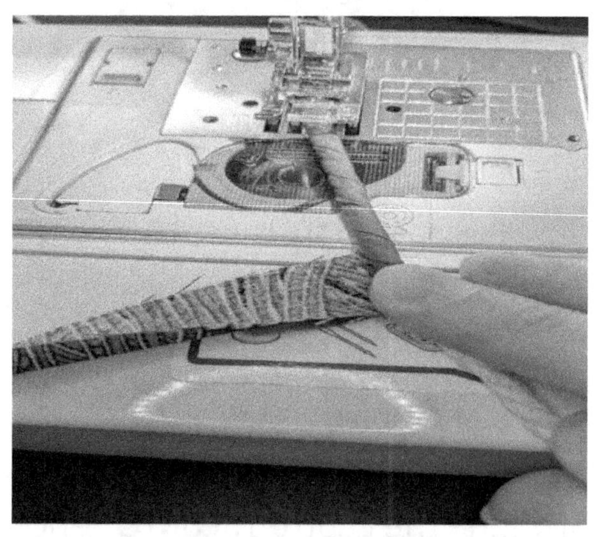

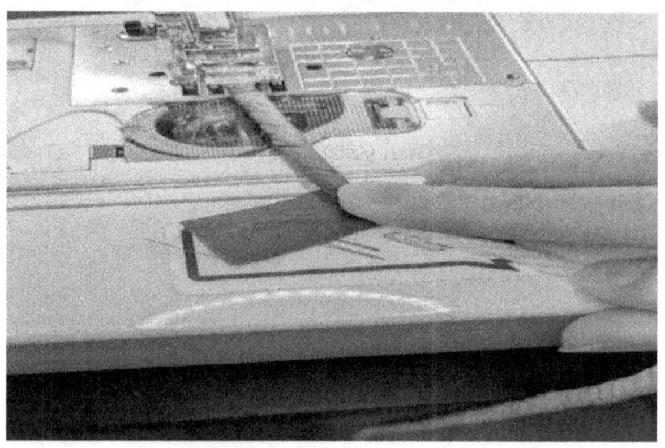

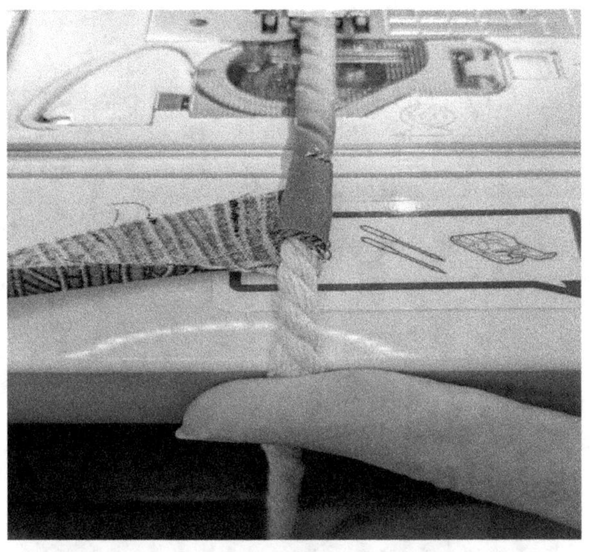

Add another strip on top of the last one's end when you reach the end of it. As you proceed, continue to wrap and stitch.

Stage 4:

Tie the rope.

I honestly have no idea how much rope I produced, but it was a lot. Making it was very soothing, and I really liked the result. The worst part was having to stop and refill the bobbin whenever it ran out.

Stage 5:

Back Piece

Utilizing a zigzag stitch, stitch the rope in the spiral pattern shown. This piece can be made to be as big or as small as you like. It will decide the bag's size. If you start stitching and discover that the majority of the spiral is on the right (like in my first illustration), just pull it out and flip it over before continuing.

Leave a six-foot rope tail at the end "long.

Stage 6:

Front Piece

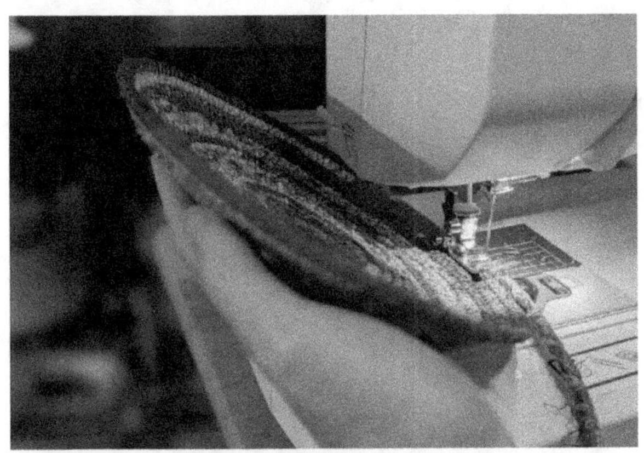

You'll make another spiral for the front, but this time, hold it up at an angle as you stitch. The rounded front will result from this.

Step 7: Strap

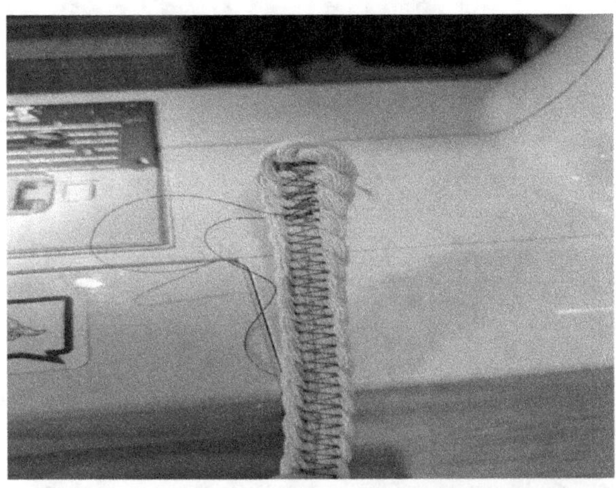

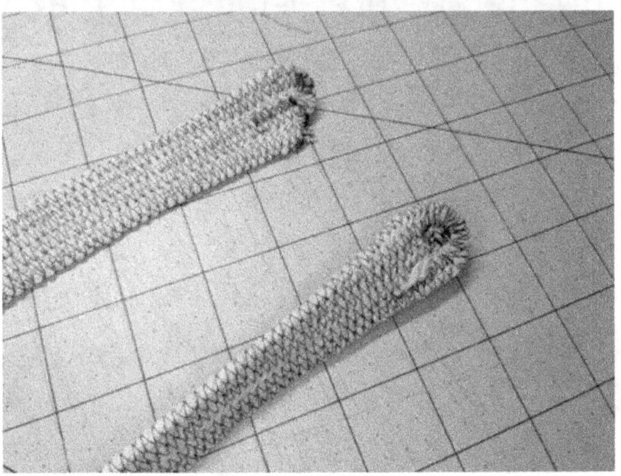

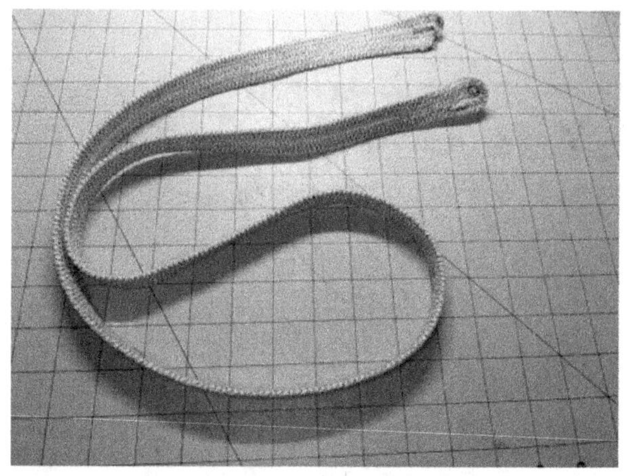

I did not cover the cotton cord in fabric before using it to make the strap. Set your strap's length aside and fold it at that length. Beginning at the fold, stitch the cord down. When you reach the end, turn it around and keep adding cord until you are satisfied with the width.

Stage 8:

Pin the front.

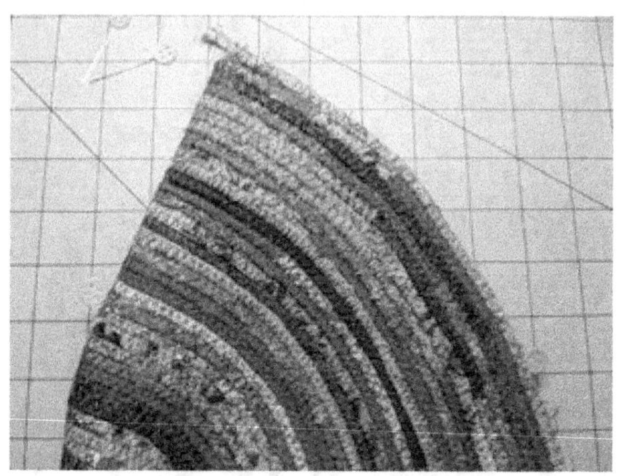

The top of the back piece must be cut down in order for it to fold over the front piece. The front piece is folded under, and the back is folded over the top. Pin the top piece's edges and center where it needs to be cut once you are satisfied with the placement.

To align the two side pins, fold the top piece in half.

Stage 9:

Cut the front.

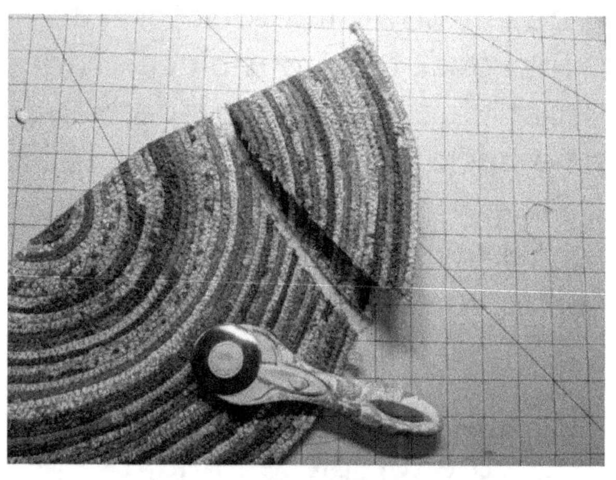

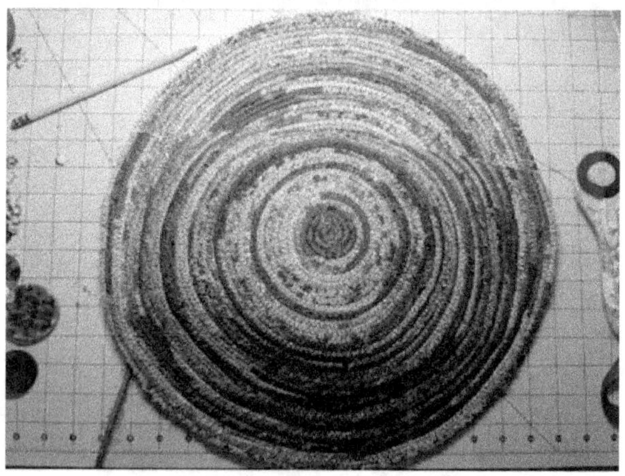

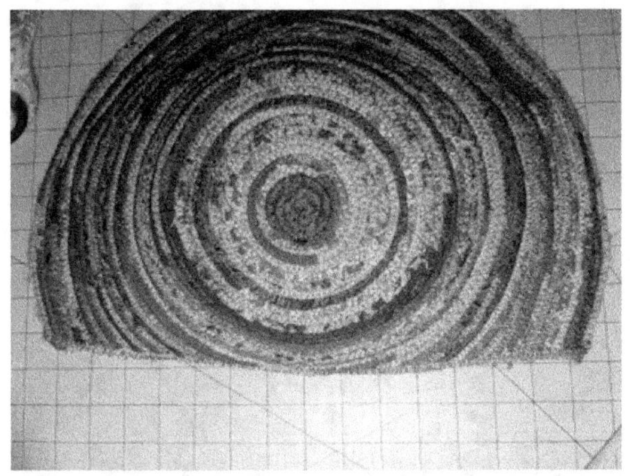

Cut through the center pins
from the side pins.

Stitch the cut edge with a piece
of cord that you have at hand.

Stage 10:

Secure the Strap

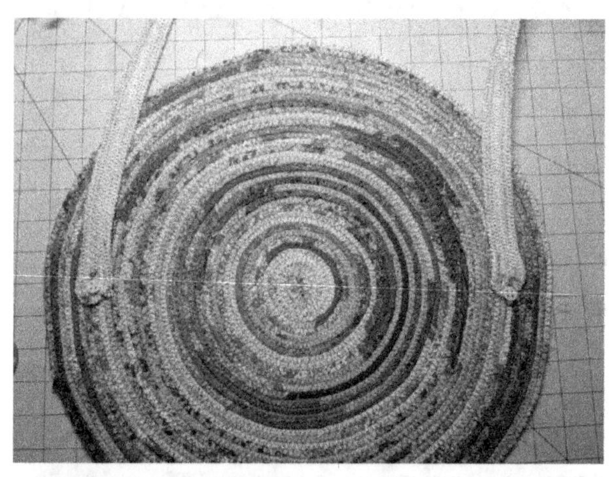

Pin the strap in place after folding the rear piece over the front. Make sure to avoid sewing above the fold.

Stage 11:

The bag's back should be folded over to meet the button in the center of the front. Using the 6 "On the end of the back piece, there is still a cord tail. Make a loop that will accommodate the button, then sew it in place as demonstrated.

Stage 12:

 button

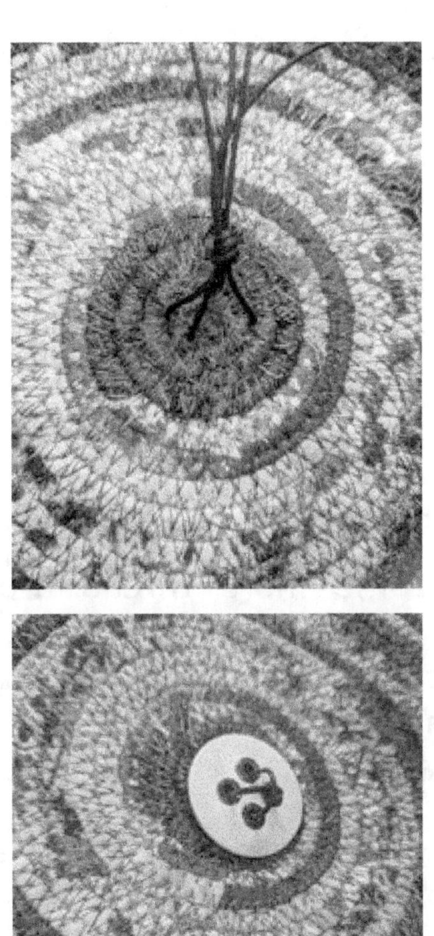

Stitch the button to the front piece's center using waxed thread. Leave a tail on the end of each piece rather than pulling the thread tight at the back. Don't tie the ends too firmly against the cloth as you tie the ends together in a knot. Make sure there is enough space to allow the front rope loop to fit behind the button.

Tie some more thread around the excess on the front as indicated to prevent the button from slipping down on this extra thread.

Stage 13:

Enjoy

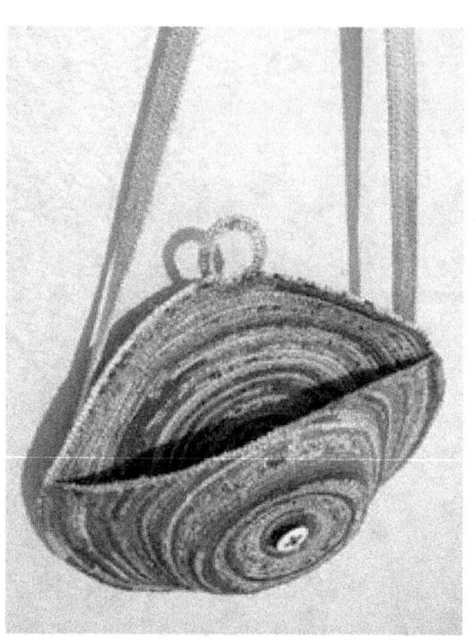

Chapter four

Another DIY Scrap Fabric Bag

This bag can be made in under two hours using leftover fabrics or pillowcases. I made use of a pillowcase from an antique store and remnants of an exquisite handloomed silk. You may get the handles from Spotlight.

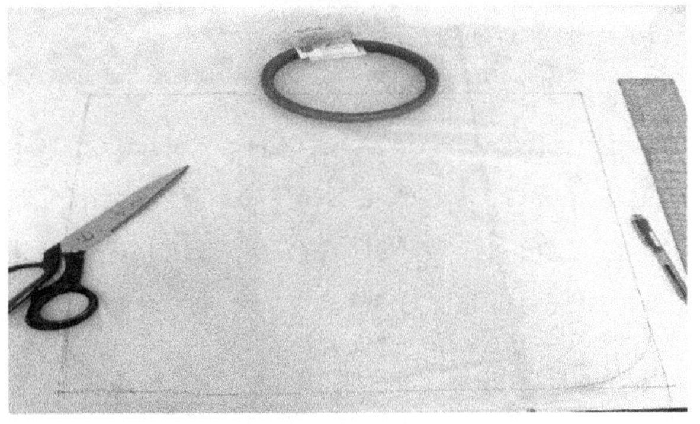

To create the desired bag form, use paper or trace and toile.

After deciding on the shape of your bag, use this pattern piece to place it over your fabric and cut out your bag.

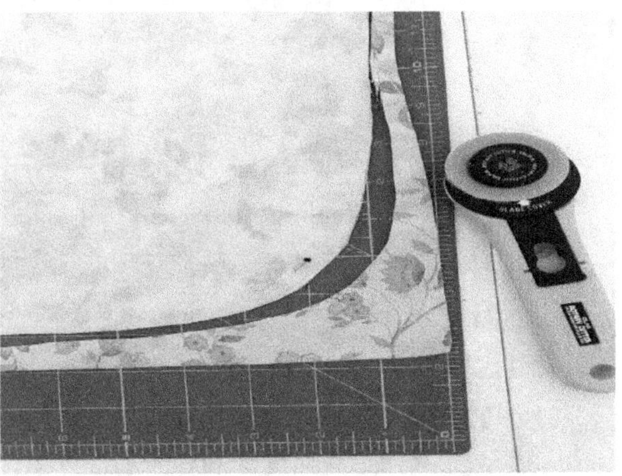

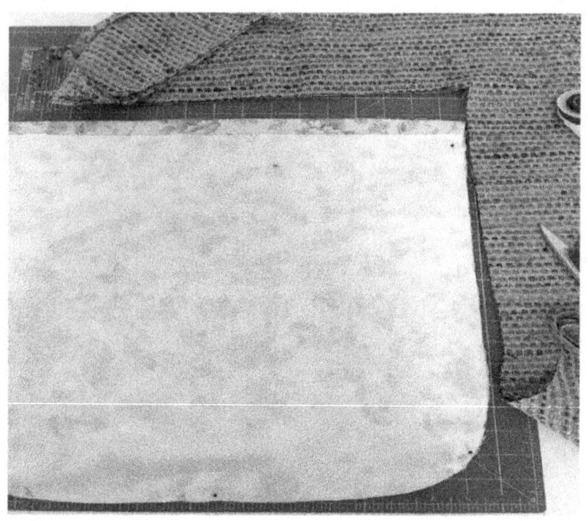

With the right sides together, stitch the pieces of outside fabric as shown below. Then, stitch the lining pieces together using the same technique, stopping 16 cm from the top to accommodate the opening "V" area. If your fabric is inclined to fray, overlock your interior seams.

4. Place the outer bag inside the lining bag and, with right sides together, sew down from the top of the bag as far as you can go into the 'V' point. Repeat the process on the other sides.

Exit the bag properly. inside the bag, press the lining. The "V"-shaped side seam area should be top stitched, then ironed flat. Then, with the wrong sides together, overlock the bag's top.

All that is left to do is

stitch the handles in. Implement the zipper foot. Enough of the bag's top edge should be folded over the handle for sewing. Through-stitch the overlocking.

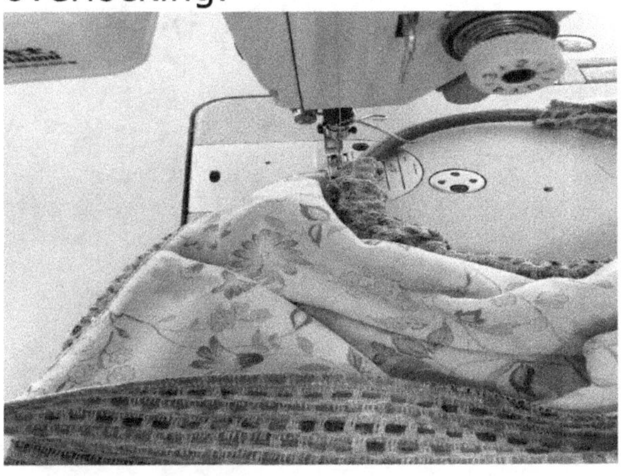

To keep the gathered section in place, give it a good steam with the iron, and you're done!

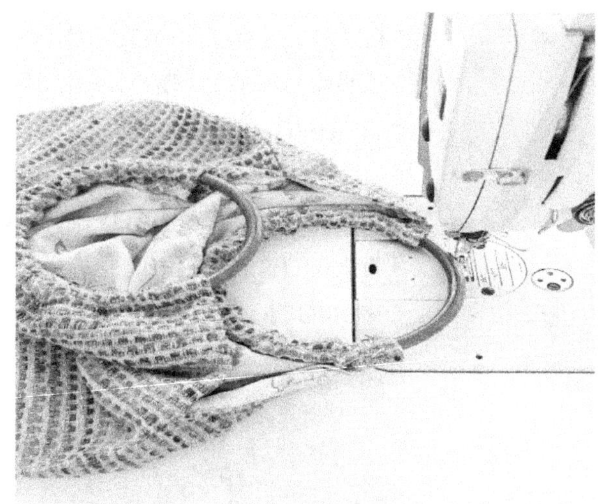